DOUNBY PRIMARY SCHOOL

WHAT WE CAN DO ABOUT

NOISE AND FUMES

Donna Bailey

WHAT WE CAN DO ABOUT

NOISE AND FUMES

Donna Bailey

Franklin Watts

London   New York   Sydney   Toronto

Original text © 1991 Donna Bailey
© 1991 Zoe Books Limited

Devised and produced by
Zoe Books Limited
15 Worthy Lane
Winchester
Hampshire SO23 7AB
England

First published in 1991
in Great Britain by
Franklin Watts Ltd
96 Leonard Street
London EC2A 4RH

First published in Australia by
Franklin Watts Australia
14 Mars Road
Lane Cove
New South Wales 2066

ISBN 0 7496 0481 6

A CIP catalogue record for this book is available from the British Library.

Printed in Italy

Design: Julian Holland Publishing Ltd
Picture researcher: Alison Renwick
Illustrators: Tony Gibbons and Tony Kenyon

Photograph acknowledgements
t = top b = bottom
Cover: Chris Fairclough Colour Library.
pp6t Robert Harding Picture Library, 6b, 7 Chris Fairclough Colour Library, 9, 11
S & R Greenhill, 12 S Terry, Harrison & Lewin/Science Photo Library, 13t Chris
Fairclough Colour Library, 13b Chris Fairclough Colour Library, 13b Robert
Harding Picture Library, 14 Glyn Davis/ICCE, 15 John Walsh/Science Photo
Library, 17t NASA/Science Photo Library, 17b Kodak Ltd/Robert Harding Picture
Library, 18 David Parker/Science Photo Library, 19t John G Ross/Robert Harding
Picture Library, 19b Magnum, 21t John Shaw/NHPA, 21b Adam Hart-Davis/
Science Photo Library, 23t Topham Picture Source, 23b Brian Brake/Science Photo
Library, 24, 25 Chris Fairclough Colour Library, 26 Hans Reinhard/Bruce Coleman
Limited, 27 Chris Fairclough Colour Library.

Contents

When people go for a walk in the countryside, they often say how much they enjoy the fresh air and the country sounds. But the country air may not be clean. In many places the air is often **polluted** by dust and **fumes**.

The sounds of the countryside may be lost in the noise made by machines and traffic. The noise of a woodcutter's chain saw drowns the songs of birds or the chirping of crickets in the grass.

Noise and fumes pollute the air even more in towns than in the countryside. If you stand by the side of any busy road and listen to the noise the traffic makes you may hear the squeal of car tyres, the roar of a motorbike engine or the rumbling of heavy trucks and buses as they pass by. The only **vehicle** that does not make a noise is a bicycle.

The air may smell of fumes from the **exhaust pipes** of cars and trucks. Smoke and fumes from homes and from power stations and factories pollute the air too. In some very large cities people are warned when there is a lot of pollution in the air. Then they may stay at home and keep their windows closed. If they go out they may wear masks, to protect them from the fumes in the air.

Measuring sound

If you drop a pebble into a pond, the ripples spread out in circles over the surface of the water. Sound travels through the air in waves like the ripples on the pond.

   The pitch of a sound depends on the number of sound waves that pass a certain point in one second. Scientists call this the **frequency** of sound. It is measured in Hertz (Hz). The higher the frequency, the more high-pitched the sound.

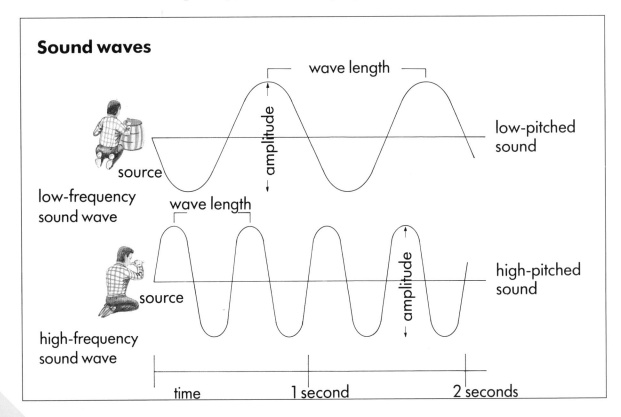

Sound waves

wave length

amplitude

low-pitched sound

source

low-frequency sound wave

wave length

amplitude

high-pitched sound

source

high-frequency sound wave

time · 1 second · 2 seconds

The loudness of a sound depends on the amplitude or height of the sound waves. Loudness, or **intensity**, of sound is measured in units called decibels (dBs).

In some countries the sound level of the traffic is checked regularly. This decibel meter in China shows that the sound level by the side of the road has reached 60 dBs.

The sounds we hear

The quietest sound that a human being can hear measures 0 dBs on a scientist's sound meter. This sound level is called the **threshold of audibility** – the point at which sound starts to be heard. Very quiet sounds, such as a pin hitting a hard floor, measure about 10 dBs.

When the sound level reaches 80 dBs, some people find that they cannot concentrate on what they are doing and the noise is annoying. They often make more mistakes in their work and may get angry more easily. The noise also makes them feel more tired.

The sound of a truck passing by may reach 90 dBs. If you have to listen to sounds every day which are as loud as 90 dBs or more it can damage your hearing and make you deaf. Many everyday sounds such as road drills, jet planes, noisy motorbikes and very loud music reach more than 90 dBs.

Sound levels

decibels

140

120

jet plane taking off

100

road drill

80

very loud music

60

heavy truck

40

a bedroom at night

a whispered conversation

20

threshold of audibility

Sounds above 120 dBs make people feel bad. This level is called the **threshold of feeling**. At 140 dBs the sound level causes people pain.

Sound levels above 155 dBs can damage machines and buildings. For example, sounds at this level can make cracks appear in metal and then make the cracks grow until the metal breaks into pieces.

People who work near loud noise have to wear earmuffs to protect their hearing, like this man with a road drill.

When sound is unwanted we call it noise, but the difference between a pleasant sound and an unwanted noise can depend on who is listening to it. A whispered conversation in a library may distract the readers and spoil their concentration.

When people need to concentrate at work, and they are using machines which reach sound levels above 80 dBs, they use earmuffs to stop the noise hurting them.

The man in the picture is using an electric saw to cut pieces of wood to the right size. He is wearing earmuffs to protect his ears from the loud whining noise of the machine.

Loud music may annoy the neighbours, even if you and your friends are enjoying it. Try to keep your music low, or use headphones. If you do wear headphones, do not wear them for long periods of time, and keep the sound level down or you may damage your own hearing. Draw your curtains at night to reduce the noise of your radio or television set.

The deafness caused by noise affects us so gradually that we do not realize how much hearing we may have lost.

Scientists wanted to know what high sound levels could do to human hearing. They tested the hearing of a group of teenagers before and after they went to a dance. At the dance, sound levels in the middle of the floor were around 110 dBs. Near the musicians the level reached 120 dBs.

The scientists found that immediately after the dance, all the teenagers had become slightly deaf. Some of them also complained of a ringing in their ears and a kind of muffled feeling. They were also extremely tired.

The air around us

Earth's **atmosphere** is made up of a mixture of gases, mainly **nitrogen** and **oxygen**. The rest is **argon**, **carbon dioxide** and water. All animals and human beings need the oxygen from the air they breathe in order to stay alive. Plants use light from the Sun, water and carbon dioxide to make food for themselves and, as they do this, they give out oxygen. This process is called **photosynthesis**.

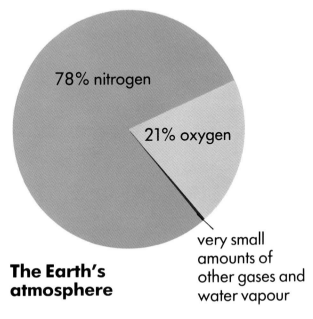

78% nitrogen

21% oxygen

very small amounts of other gases and water vapour

The Earth's atmosphere

Rainforests and grasslands take in large amounts of carbon dioxide during photosynthesis. If they are destroyed, the amount of carbon dioxide in the air increases. Sometimes forests are destroyed by burning, which gives out more carbon dioxide into the atmosphere and pollutes the air with smoke. Some farmers burn rainforests to clear the land so that they can grow food, such as the banana crop in the picture.

You can use your senses to find out if the air is polluted. You can see some kinds of air pollution, like fumes from factory chimneys and exhaust fumes from cars and trucks. You cannot see some other air pollutants, but you can smell some of them, like the gas **sulphur dioxide**. This gas goes into the Earth's atmosphere wherever fuels such as coal or oil are burned.

Power stations and factories use these fuels. One way to help reduce air pollution would be to cut down the amount of fuel used to make goods. Factories use less fuel to make goods from recycled materials. You can help prevent air pollution by taking metal cans, glass and paper to the recycling centres near you.

The ozone level

Scientists divide the atmosphere stretching high above the Earth into layers. One of these layers is the **stratosphere**, where there is a gas called **ozone**.

The ozone in the stratosphere is important for all living things on Earth because it blocks out most of the **ultraviolet rays** from the Sun. Too much ultraviolet light is harmful to all living things. It can damage people's eyes and cause skin cancer.

Scientists have been making regular checks on the ozone level for many years. In 1986 photographs taken from space showed that there was much less ozone over Antarctica than before. Scientists found a very big hole in the ozone layer. It was as big as the USA and as high as Mount Everest.

The main layers of the Earth's atmosphere

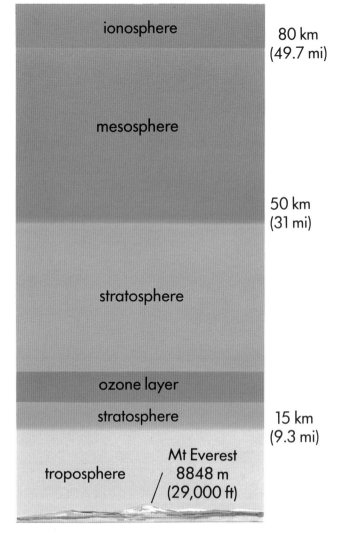

ionosphere — 80 km (49.7 mi)

mesosphere

— 50 km (31 mi)

stratosphere

ozone layer

stratosphere — 15 km (9.3 mi)

troposphere — Mt Everest 8848 m (29,000 ft)

surface of the Earth

Satellite photographs like this one on the right, taken a year later, showed that the hole in the ozone layer had grown bigger. Antarctica is outlined in white. The deep blue, purple, black and pink colours mark the areas where the hole in the ozone layer is getting larger.

Many scientists think that the ozone has been destroyed partly by chemicals called chlorofluorocarbons (CFCs), which we make on Earth.

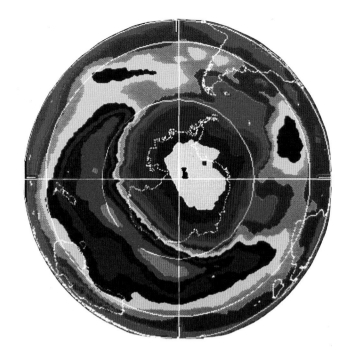

We use CFCs in many things, from refrigerators to furniture. We also use them in some aerosol cans, to help squirt out the contents. CFCs are added to plastic to make the spongy foam that is sometimes used for egg cartons and containers for hamburgers.

If you are helping with the shopping, check that the spray cans you choose do not contain CFCs. A pump action spray works just as well. When you choose food in cartons or containers look for the ones which are not made of spongy plastic.

Fumes in the air

Most of the fumes which pollute the air are made when fuel or rubbish is burned. Smoke, containing soot, dust and gases goes into the air.

Sometimes when bright sunlight shines on air which is full of gases from car exhausts and power stations a **photochemical smog** is made. In some big cities, like Los Angeles in the picture below, the smog turns the air a light brownish colour.

Smog can cause lung damage, so some people wear masks to cut down the amount of smog they breathe in.

The petrol fumes from car exhausts contain lead. Lead is poisonous and even small amounts can harm growing children and may damage their brains. Most of the lead in children's bodies is breathed in from petrol fumes. Many service stations sell unleaded petrol. This is petrol which does not have extra lead added to it. Perhaps your family car can run on unleaded petrol.

If your family are planning to take you for a trip in the car, ask them if you could all take a walk or a bicycle ride instead. It could be more fun, and you will not pollute the air with exhaust fumes.

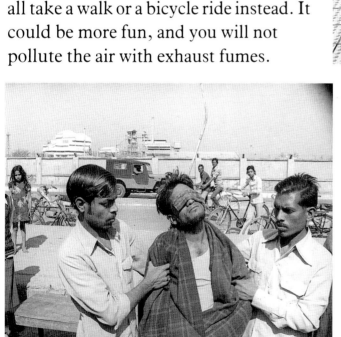

Sometimes the gases which pollute the air have escaped from a factory. When there was an accident at a factory in Bhopal, India, a poisonous gas escaped into the air. It killed more than 2000 people who lived nearby, and thousands more people were injured. Many people had to be treated for damage to their eyes, skin and lungs.

Acid rain

When factories and power stations burn fuels such as coal and oil, the gas sulphur dioxide escapes into the atmosphere. Car exhaust fumes have a gas called **nitrogen dioxide** in them. If either of these gases mixes with water droplets in the air, a chemical change takes place. Acids are formed, which may fall back to Earth as acid rain or acid snow.

The wind can blow the polluted air a long way from the factories which made the gases in the first place. Governments in many countries now have laws to cut down the air pollution which leads to acid rain.

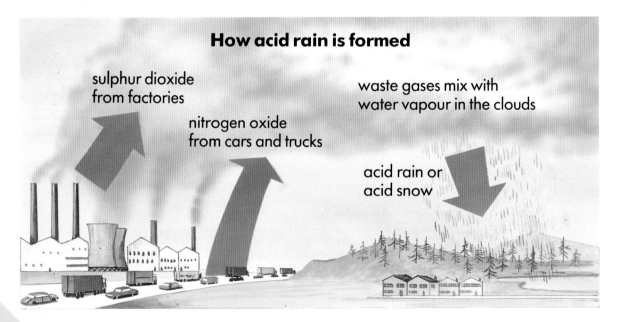

How acid rain is formed

sulphur dioxide from factories

nitrogen oxide from cars and trucks

waste gases mix with water vapour in the clouds

acid rain or acid snow

Acid rain damages leaves and kills plants. The effect of acid rain on the forests in Germany was first noticed in the 1970s. The needles on Silver Fir trees became discoloured and then fell off. The damage spread from the lower branches to the top of the trees, until only the bare trunks were left. Today many trees in Europe and North America have been damaged by acid rain. The fir trees in the picture have died from the effects of acid rain. They are in North Carolina, USA.

Acid rain is also slowly destroying the plant and animal life in the freshwater lakes throughout Europe and North America. About one-fifth of all the lakes in Sweden are now so acid that only the hardiest kinds of plants and animals can live in them.

Acid rain can also damage stonework and statues, as you can see in the picture.

The greenhouse effect

The Sun warms the Earth's surface. Some of the heat then **radiates** from the Earth into the atmosphere. Some gases in the atmosphere, such as carbon dioxide and **methane**, trap some of this heat and make the atmosphere warmer. Then the heat radiates back to the Earth. This is called the greenhouse effect, because the gases in the air stop some of the heat escaping, just like the glass in a greenhouse.

The amount of carbon dioxide in the atmosphere has been increasing rapidly over the last 20 years, as more and more factories and cars pollute the air with this gas.

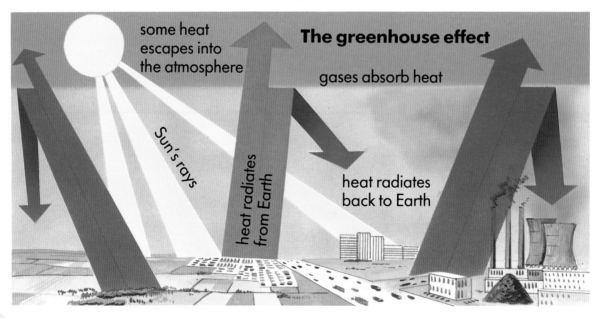

some heat escapes into the atmosphere

The greenhouse effect

gases absorb heat

Sun's rays

heat radiates from Earth

heat radiates back to Earth

Some scientists think that if the amounts of carbon dioxide and other gases which trap heat continue to increase, the world will get warmer. This is called **global warming**. The average temperatures around the world may rise by as much as 4°C during the next 60 years.

Such a change in the Earth's temperature could mean that the weather and climate in many different parts of the world would change.

Some places would have more rainfall and high winds, while other places would become drier and hotter. Scientists think that parts of the USA would have less rain, and so crops, like the cotton crop in the picture above, would die.

Water in the seas and oceans would expand with the rise in temperature and ice around the north and south poles would melt, adding more water. Farmlands in parts of Bangladesh and India would be flooded, like the fields in the picture on the left. Parts of Florida in the USA and East Anglia in Britain would be under water.

Cleaning the air

Clean air is important for all living things on our planet. Many countries have laws to control the air pollution from power stations and factories.

You can help to clean the air too. If you are helping to clear garden rubbish, ask if you can make it into **compost** instead of burning it. Find out if there is a tree planting programme in your area. Planting more trees in parks and play areas will help reduce the amount of carbon dioxide in the air.

In many places there are shops which sell food and other goods which have been grown or made nearby. The vehicles which bring them to the shops have not had far to travel. They have not used much fuel, so the air pollution is less. When you are out shopping with your family, try to choose goods which are made or grown nearby.

You can see that the goods at the market in the picture above are not packed in plastic cartons or containers. If you live near a market, ask your family if you can go shopping there. Remember to take shopping bags with you, so that you do not need to use new boxes and bags from the market stalls. Waste containers and cartons are often burned, which adds to the pollution in the air.

Finding out about noise pollution

1 Make a list of all the sounds you can hear for ten minutes in the morning, ten minutes at midday and ten minutes in the evening. Compare your list with a friend's. How many of the sounds are the same?

2 Make a sound survey. Ask your friends which sounds they like most and which sounds they dislike. Can you group the sounds into natural, musical and mechanical sounds?

3 Try wearing earmuffs at home for part of the day. What happens when you wear them? What happens when you take them off?

4 If you have double glazing at home or in school, what difference does it make to the sounds you can hear when you open the window?

Sound Survey	1=natural sound		2=mechanical sound		3=musical sound			
Name	Likes	1	2	3	Dislikes	1	2	3
Anna	bird song	✓		✓	her baby brother crying	✓		
	cats purring	✓						
James					heavy trucks passing by		✓	

Finding out about air pollution

1 How many times do you travel by car every week? Make a list of where you go by car. Could you have got there by walking, by bike, or on a bus or train?

2 How dirty is the air near your home or school? One way you can measure air pollution is to leave some pieces of shiny white plastic in different parts of the house or school and in the garden or park. Check them at the end of the week. Which piece of plastic is the dirtiest? Can you work out why?

3 Do a survey of cars belonging to the families of children in your class. Find out which cars use unleaded petrol.

Glossary

argon: one of the gases found in small amounts in the Earth's atmosphere.

atmosphere: the mixture of gases, dust and water droplets which surround the Earth.

carbon dioxide: a gas made of carbon and oxygen.

compost: rotted plants which are used to enrich the soil.

exhaust pipe: the pipe from a car engine that takes away the waste gases.

frequency: the number of waves which pass a fixed point each second.

fumes: smoke and gases which are usually made when something is burned.

global warming: a rise in the temperature on the surface of the Earth and in the lower atmosphere.

intensity: the strength or amount of something.

methane: a gas given off when living things rot, and found underground, especially in coal mines.

nitrogen: one of the main gases of the Earth's atmosphere.

nitrogen dioxide: a gas made from nitrogen and oxygen. It mixes with water droplets in the atmosphere to form nitric acid, which falls as acid rain.

oxygen: one of the main gases of the Earth's atmosphere which is needed by most living things to stay alive.

ozone: a gas made of small particles of oxygen. A layer of ozone at a high level in the atmosphere shields the Earth from the harmful rays of the Sun.

photochemical smog: the air pollution which happens when sunlight changes the fumes given off by burning petrol and oil.

photosynthesis: the way in which plants use the light from the Sun to turn carbon dioxide and water into food.

pollute: to spoil or destroy the air, water or our environment.

radiate: to send out rays such as heat or light.

stratosphere: a layer of the Earth's atmosphere about 10 km (6 mi) from the surface of the Earth. The ozone layer is in the stratosphere.

sulphur dioxide: a gas made from sulphur and oxygen, which is given off when some things are burned. It mixes with water droplets in the atmosphere to form sulphuric acid, which may then fall as acid rain.

threshold of audibility: the sound level at which human beings can just hear sounds.

threshold of feeling: the level at which sounds start to become uncomfortable for human beings to hear.

ultraviolet rays: invisible rays of light from the Sun which can be harmful to plants and other living things.

vehicle: any kind of transport which can move people or goods from place to place.

Index